Tattoo Artist

VIRGINIA LOH-HAGAN

⊙ 45th Parallel Press

Published in the United States of America by Cherry Lake Publishing
Ann Arbor, Michigan
www.cherrylakepublishing.com

Content Adviser: Rob Lloyd, tattooer, The Black Rose, Waterford MI
Reading Adviser: Marla Conn, ReadAbility, Inc.
Book Design: Felicia Macheske

Photo Credits: © Ronald Sumners / Shutterstock.com, cover, 1; © Bill Putnam / ZUMAPRESS / Newscom, 5;
© Rob Lloyd / The Black Rose, 6; © Mikhail_Kayl / Shutterstock.com, 9; © jacomstephens / iStock, 11; © Todor
Rusinov / Shutterstock.com, 13; © Everett Historical / Shutterstock.com, 15; © Pavel L Photo and Video /
Shutterstock.com, 16-17; © LukaTDB / Shutterstock.com, 19; © Heritage Image Partnership Ltd / Alamy, 21;
© Todor Rusinov / Shutterstock.com, 23; © Chronicle / Alamy, 25; © Ron Chapple studios / Thinkstock, 27;
© Zoonar RF / Thinkstock, 28; © ARENA Creative / Shutterstock.com, cover and multiple interior pages;
© oculo / Shutterstock.com, multiple interior pages; © Denniro / Shutterstock.com, multiple interior pages;
© PhotoHouse / Shutterstock.com, multiple interior pages; © Miloje / Shutterstock.com, multiple interior pages

45th Parallel Press is an imprint of Cherry Lake Publishing.

Library of Congress Cataloging-in-Publication Data

Loh-Hagan, Virginia.
  Tattoo artist / Virginia Loh-Hagan.
      pages cm — (Odd jobs)
  Includes bibliographical references and index.
  ISBN 978-1-63470-031-3 (hardcover) — ISBN 978-1-63470-085-6 (pdf) — ISBN 978-1-63470-058-0 (pbk.)
— ISBN 978-1-63470-112-9 (ebook)
1. Tattoo artists. 2. Tattooing. I. Title.

GT2345.L65 2016
391.6'5—dc23

2015008292

Cherry Lake Publishing would like to acknowledge the work of The Partnership for 21st Century Skills.
Please visit www.p21.org for more information.

Printed in the United States of America
Corporate Graphics Inc.

Artists clean the needles with water. This is done during the tattooing. It's also done during color changes.

Some tattoo artists use a stencil machine. It uses special paper. Tattoo artists put the special paper on the skin. The design comes off the paper. It sticks to the skin.

Tattoos are open cuts. Tattoo artists tell clients to be careful. They clean the area. They give clients bandages. They give them healing cream.

Magnums are needles used for coloring and shading.

CHAPTER 3

To Be Ink Masters

Who is Charles Wagner? Why do people want to become tattoo artists? What are some things tattoo artists specialize in? What do people need to do in order to become a tattoo artist?

Charles Wagner was an early American tattoo artist. He helped develop tattooing. He changed how people looked. He tattooed women's lips, cheeks, and eyebrows. He also tattooed horses and dogs. This was so they couldn't be stolen.

RAND McNALLY

DISCOVERY ATLAS OF
DINOSAURS
& PREHISTORIC
CREATURES

Rand McNally for Kids™
Books•Maps•Atlases

Discovery Atlas of Dinosaurs and Prehistoric Creatures

General manager: Russell L. Voisin
Managing editor: Jon M. Leverenz
Editor: Elizabeth Fagan Adelman
Production editor: Laura C. Schmidt
Manufacturing planner: Marianne Abraham

Discovery Atlas of Dinosaurs and Prehistoric Creatures
Copyright © 1994 by Rand McNally & Company
Published and printed in the United States of America

Photograph and art credits
American Museum of Natural History, courtesy Department of Library
Services: Page 46 Monsasaur/No. 2425. Dinosaur National
Monument/National Park Service: 13 Fossils; 14 Apatosaurus; 34
Fossils. Field Museum of Natural History: 28 Cynognathus/No.
CK22T; 35 Brachiosaurus cast/No. GN86846; 37 Stegosaurus/No.
CK31T; 38–39 Jurassic seas/No. CK34T; 39 Jurassic flyers/No.
CK39T; 56–57 Eocene mammals/No. CK46T. Florissant Fossil Beds
National Monument: 14 Robber Fly, Fish; 27 Shrub fossil. Milwaukee
Public Museum: 22 Silurian reef; 56–57 Great Plains mammals. NASA:
58 Greenland. Peter Trusler, artist: 29 Hatchling, reproduced courtesy
Australia Post; 47 Australian dinosaurs, reproduced courtesy Australia
Post. Professor Hans Fricke/Max Planck Institut für
Verhaltersphysiologie: 24 Coelocanth. Rand McNally's *America*: 30
Appalachians. Smithsonian Institution: 63 Basilosaurus Photo No.
93-2697. United States Geological Survey: 12–13 Grand Canyon; 51
Meteor Crater. William K. Hartmann: 4–5 Young solar system; 6–7
Earth and Moon; 50–51 Impact Sequence.

Reddy, Francis, 1959-
    [Rand McNally children's atlas of earth through time]
    Rand McNally discovery atlas of dinosaurs & prehistoric creatures
/ [writer, Francis Reddy ; illustrators, Jan Wills, Pat Ortega].
        p. cm.
    Pbk. adaptation of: Rand McNally children's atlas of earth through
time / Francis Reddy.
    Includes index.
    ISBN 0-528-83677-3
    1. Historical geology—Juvenile literature. [1. Historical
geology.] I. Wills, Jan, ill. II. Ortega, Pat, ill. III. Title.
IV. Title: Discovery atlas of dinosaurs and prehistoric creatures.
QE28.3.R43   1994
551.7—dc20   93-43086
                                                 CIP
                                                 AC

Contents

Beginnings

Earth's Birth

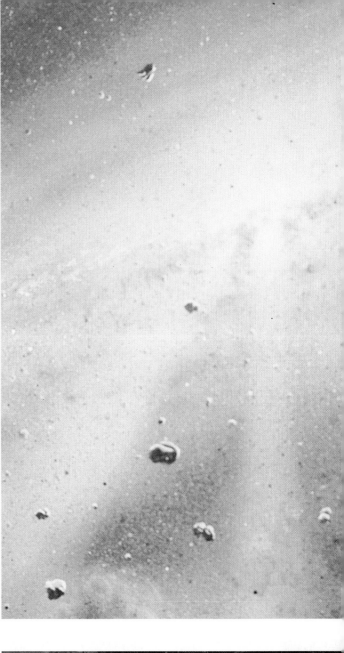

About 4.6 billion years ago, a giant dust cloud gave birth to our solar system. Inside this cloud, a small pocket of gas and dust started to cave in, or collapse. Once it started, the cloud became smaller and denser. It spun faster and faster as it collapsed, and the speed of the spin flattened it into a disk. Deep within the center, where material was squeezed the most, a ball of gas became ever hotter and denser. After a few million years, reactions within the disk's center released great amounts of energy. Our Sun was born.

At the same time, the planets were starting to form. Tiny dust grains collided and stuck together, forming pebbles, boulders, and larger bodies. Eventually these bodies grew large enough for their gravity to attract other material to them. The planets we know were built up by sweeping up the debris in the solar system.

The four planets closest to the Sun have hard, rocky surfaces. Mercury, Venus, Earth, and Mars are the four *terrestrial* planets. The next four planets are mostly gas. These planets are Jupiter, Saturn, Uranus, and Neptune. The last planet, Pluto, is thought to be mostly ice.

Between Mars and Jupiter, tens of thousands of chunks of rock and metal called *asteroids* orbit the Sun. Over the long history of the solar system, asteroids have hit the planets and their moons many times. An asteroid that reaches Earth's surface is called a *meteorite*.

Some 4.6 billion years ago, a small pocket of gas and dust began collapsing. Spinning ever faster as it collapsed, the cloud flattened into a disk. For the next ten million years, a ball of gas in the center of the cloud grew smaller, denser, and hotter.

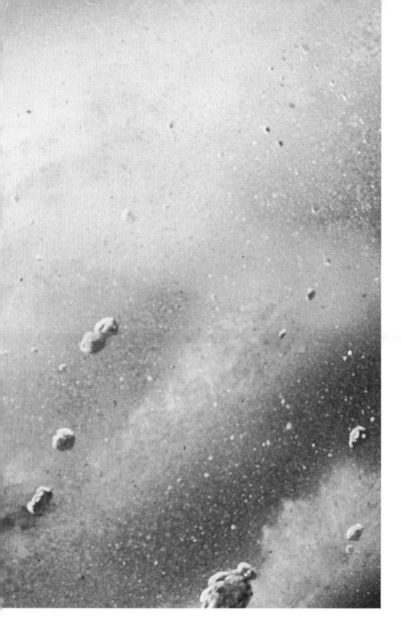

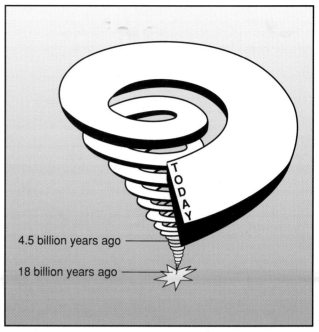

The solar system formed about 4.5 billion years ago.

The young solar system was filled with gas, dust, and small rocky bodies. By colliding and joining together, these objects built the planets of the solar system.

The ball grew hot enough to produce its own energy from nuclear reactions. The Sun was born. Matter in the disk slowly clumped together, forming the cores of the planets.

Over the next 100 million years, the planets swept up much of the solar system's rocky debris.

A Hostile World

The young Earth grew as its gravity drew rocky debris into it. The collisions created enough heat to keep the early Earth in a state we can hardly imagine today. Our planet was a soupy, glowing ball of melted rock and metal. Earth boiled at a temperature near 2,500° F (1,370° C).

Sometime early in its history, Earth was joined by its partner in space, the Moon. Just how this happened no one knows for sure. Many scientists believe that the Moon was formed when a large body from space crashed into Earth. Such an impact may have nearly shattered the young Earth. It would have

blasted large amounts of rock into space. Some of the rock would have begun to orbit around the planet. Many believe that our Moon was born when this material collected into a single body.

Within 100 million years after Earth was formed, something happened that forever changed it. Melted drops of iron

At one time, the young Earth was a great glowing ball of melted rock and metal. Earth grew as its gravity attracted smaller bodies to it. Heat from the impacts helped keep it in a molten state.

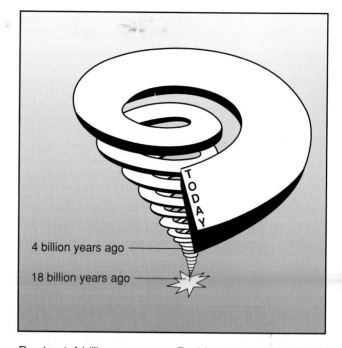

4 billion years ago

18 billion years ago

By about 4 billion years ago, Earth's core and crust had formed. The oldest rocks ever discovered are 3.96 billion years old.

Many scientists believe the Moon was born in a cosmic collision. The young Earth may have nearly shattered when an object the size of Mars smashed into it. Debris was thrown into orbit around Earth and later collected to form the Moon.

and other heavy chemical materials slowly sank toward Earth's center. The ball of liquid iron they formed became the Earth's *core*. The core is still mostly liquid today. Its heat drives volcanoes and other activities that change Earth's surface.

Just as the heavy materials sank into the center of Earth, lighter materials floated toward the surface. They collected to form Earth's outer layer, called its *crust*.

This early crust could not have lasted long. Collisions with the rocky debris of the young solar system must have smashed it many times. But strong, stable rocks such as granite gradually formed. The continents rest on these rocks today.

With the creation of a rocky crust, the first volcanoes erupted. Huge outpourings of melted rock, or *lava*, thickened the crust. This in turn helped create our atmosphere. Gases locked in the interior of Earth began to bubble up to the surface. Carbon dioxide, methane, and water vapor streamed out of erupting volcanoes.

Water vapor was very important. High in the atmosphere it condensed into droplets of water. Forming thick clouds, it fell to the young Earth as heavy rain. When the rain hit hot spots on the surface, the water evaporated again. Rising into the sky, it condensed, then fell again.

Slowly, Earth's surface cooled. Water flowed across the landscape and collected in the low places of the crust. The first oceans formed.

Lightning and strong *ultraviolet light* from the Sun provided energy to make new chemicals. Some of them, those known as *amino acids*, are part of all life on Earth. Over a long period of time, the molecules built from these chemicals became more and more complex.

The Moon looms over lava pools on the young, fiery Earth. Lava and gases bubble to Earth's surface, thickening its crust and creating an atmosphere.

One day, perhaps within some quiet tidal pool, chance combinations created a molecule with a curious spiral shape. This molecule had a special feature: it could make copies of itself. Less than a billion years after Earth's formation, *DNA* had formed. Today DNA can be found in nearly all living things. Created in a world very different from the one we know today, it is nothing less than the blueprint for life on Earth.

The Living Planet

About 240 million years ago, nearly all the continents were joined in a vast supercontinent named *Pangaea*.

The Faces of Earth

The Earth's surface remains restless even today. The crust is not a single mass, but is broken into a dozen or so large, rigid slabs called *tectonic plates*. These plates slide against each other at speeds of about 0.4 to 4 inches (1 to 10 centimeters) per year. The plates are thicker under the continents than under the ocean, but they average about fifty miles (eighty kilometers) thick. They are formed out of the Earth's crust and the very top part of the Earth's *mantle*. The mantle is the part of the Earth beween its crust and its core.

The plates slide atop a layer of the deeper mantle. Here the rock is partly molten. It is hot enough and weak enough to swirl as heat rises from the Earth's center. These swirling currents nudge the plates. Where the plates grind

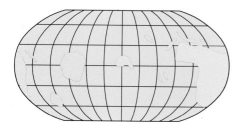

Earth's surface as it appeared about 510 million years ago. . .

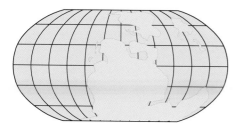

. . .about 240 million years ago. . .

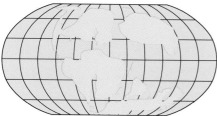

. . .about 135 million years ago. . .

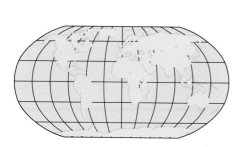

. . .and as it appears today.

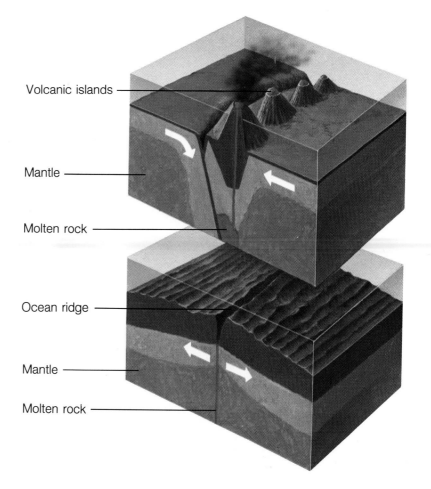

The movement of *tectonic plates* causes changes in the Earth's crust. Volcanoes erupt above hot spots where one plate rides into another (top). The oceans widen as the plates spread away from ocean ridges (bottom). The arrangement of Earth's landmasses changes over time.

against each other, pressure builds up. Sometimes it becomes so great that the rock shatters, causing an earthquake. Near the edge of a plate, molten rock sometimes rises to the surface, creating volcanoes.

These moving plates also change the size and arrangement of land. Hot rock erupts at undersea ridges and widens the oceans. Plates may collide and pile up against each other, forming mountains. Over millions of years, these events have slowly changed the face of our Earth. For example, at one time nearly all the continents were joined together as a single landmass!

The Story of Rocks

The record of Earth's past is held within its rocks. Over the past four hundred years, scientists have struggled to learn just how to read that record.

People have long collected strange or interesting rocks. Sometimes rocks far from the sea would be shaped like shells or underwater plants. Today, such rocks are known to be the remains of plants or animals and are called *fossils*. As early as 1500, many scientists argued that fossils were exactly what they appeared to be. For the next hundred years, scientists worked to figure out exactly how plant and animal remains turned into rock.

In 1666, a Danish physician named Nicolaus Steno was living in Italy. One day, local fishermen brought him a large white shark they had caught. Steno no-

Stripes along the walls of Arizona's Grand Canyon show layers of rock that formed at different times. Long ago, when the area was under a vast sea, sediments sank to the sea floor and turned into rock. The Colorado River later carved a path through the rock, creating the canyon and revealing its layered walls.

Scientists at Dinosaur National Monument in Utah carefully remove the jumbled remains of ancient animals from sandstone. The wall contains over two thousand fossil bones.

ticed that the shark's triangular teeth were very much like triangular rocks known as "tonguestones." He thought that tonguestones really *were* the teeth of ancient sharks. But how could sharks' teeth turn into solid rock?

Steno suggested that plants and animals got trapped within the silt and sand that fell to the bottom of lakes, rivers, and oceans. Over a long period of time,

the sand and silt hardened, turning into rock. The plant and animal parts inside it kept their shape as they hardened too.

The type of rock Steno considered is called *sedimentary* rock. When these rocks form, they collect in layers. The oldest layers rest on the bottom and the youngest layers sit on top. The discovery of this kind of rock helped scientists learn about Earth's history.

Buried for 145 million years, the massive shoulder blade of an *Apatosaurus* and other fossils are at last unearthed.

The best examples of sedimentary rock are the banded walls of the Grand Canyon. The flow of the Colorado River has cut through deeper and deeper layers of rock. Rock layers at the bottom of the canyon formed first, and higher layers formed later.

Such orderly rock layers, or *strata*, are not common. The slow changes of the Earth's surface have turned organized layers of rock into a confusing jumble. Scientists have tried to put together an overall picture of Earth's past from these layers. But the jumble of layers from all different times has made it very difficult.

Fossils provided a key. When scientists found the same fossils in rocks in different places, they knew the rocks in those places probably formed at the same time. Also, fossils found in some rock layers looked very different from living creatures, so scientists knew the fossils were very old. Fossils in other rocks looked a lot like plants and animals that were still living. This meant the remains were not very old. So fossils gave scien-

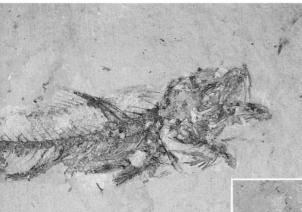

Preserved by the ash of an erupting volcano, this fish helps tell the story of Earth's past.

The *robber fly* buzzed around Florissant, Colorado, some 35 million years ago.

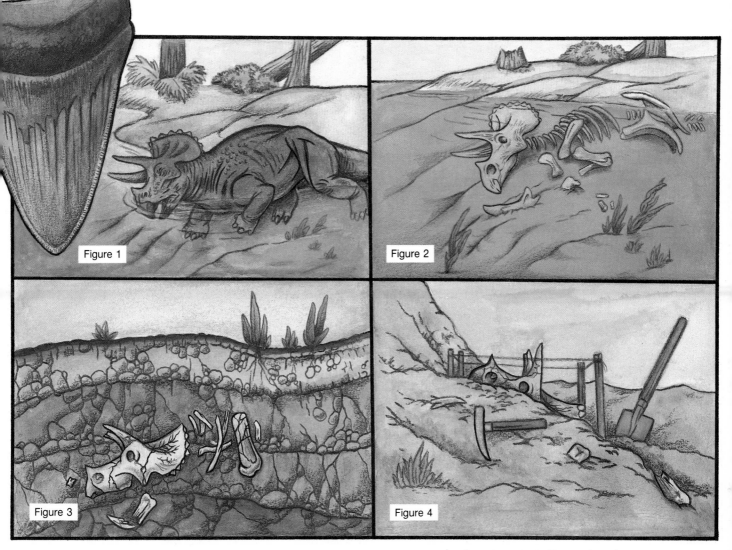

The fossil of an ancient shark's tooth (upper left) looks very much like the tooth of a living shark. The series above shows how fossils form. A dinosaur dies in a river or a lake and sinks to the muddy bottom (figure 1). Layers of sand and silt bury the dinosaur. Its flesh decays, but the sediment layers help preserve its bones (figure 2). The lake slowly evaporates over millions of years and the lake bed turns into rock (figure 3). Eventually, wind and rain wear away parts of this sedimentary rock, revealing the fossilized bones of the dinosaur (figure 4).

tists a way to identify the ages of rock layers around the world.

Using fossils, geologists divided the Earth's past into four sections called *eras*. The eras are named the Cenozoic (meaning "recent life"), Mesozoic ("middle life"), Paleozoic ("ancient life"), and the Precambrian ("before the Cambrian Period of the Paleozoic Era"). Each era was further divided into shorter *periods*.

Today, geologists can figure out the ages of rocks by studying the *radioactive* materials within them. The oldest rocks ever found on Earth, discovered in Canada in 1989, are 3.96 billion years old. Rocks collected from the Moon are between 3.7 billion and 4.5 billion years old. And the oldest signs of life on Earth were molded into Australian rocks some 3.5 billion years ago.

The Precambrian Era

First Life

Within Earth's first billion years, its crust cooled and turned solid. Vast oceans filled the lowest areas, and air filled with poisonous gas surrounded the planet. Intense ultraviolet sunlight baked the young Earth's barren, rocky surface.

Most life today could not survive such conditions. Yet this is where life began. By about 3.4 billion years ago, simple single-celled plants such as *blue-green algae* probably filled the oceans. These plants made their own food by using the energy in sunlight. This process, called *photosynthesis*, is used by nearly all plants today.

Ancient rock formations from this time called *stromatolites* reveal algae communities. The sticky mats of algae trapped sand and mud to create these layered rocks. Stromatolites dominate the fossil record for the next 2.7 billion years and exist in small numbers today. Simple animals such as sponges, worms, and jellyfish-like creatures appeared about 700 million years ago. The explosion of life on Earth was underway.

Single-celled life forms, such as these bacteria, appeared very early in Earth's history.

Worm-like *Spriggina* wriggled across the sea floor 700 million years ago.

The worm *Dickinsonia* looks a little like a pancake. Its fossils were found in the rocks of Flinders Range in South Australia.

Jellyfish-like *Ediacara* swam through the seas of the late Precambrian Era.

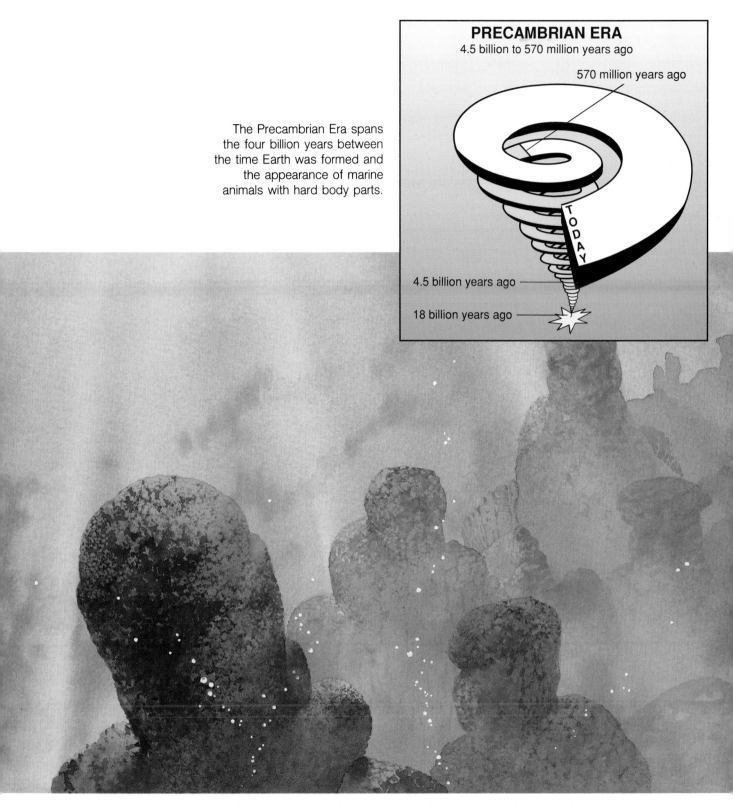

PRECAMBRIAN ERA
4.5 billion to 570 million years ago

570 million years ago

TODAY

4.5 billion years ago

18 billion years ago

The Precambrian Era spans the four billion years between the time Earth was formed and the appearance of marine animals with hard body parts.

Sticky mats of *blue-green algae* create large dome-shaped structures called *stromatolites*. Mud particles trapped on the mat's upper surface become solid, layered domes. Stromatolites dominate the fossil record between three billion and 700 million years ago, and a few live today.

Creatures in Paleozoic seas ranged from simple forms like sponges and corals (bottom) to advanced fish like sharks (center). This scene represents the variety of animals that appeared in the Paleozoic Era—they did not all live at the same time.

The Paleozoic Era

The Animals of the Ancient Sea

Rocks from the Cambrian Period, some 570 million years old, reveal an incredible variety of life. Fossils of earlier creatures—such as worms and jellyfish—appear rarely because their soft bodies did not preserve well. But at the close of the Precambrian Era, the first animals with hard external skeletons began to appear. Since their bodies were easier to preserve, Cambrian rocks contain many of their fossils.

Some of the most common creatures were the *trilobites*. These oval-shaped animals usually lived on the sea floor, scurring through the mud to find food. They ranged in size from less than an inch (2.5 centimeters) to well over a foot (31 centimeters). If threatened, they

The *crinoid*, or sea lily, is an animal, not a plant. Hairs in the cup move water and food into the creature's mouth. Most species died out at the end of the Paleozoic Era, but some survive today.

Brachiopods are among the most common Paleozoic fossils and still exist today. Like clams, they protect their soft bodies by building a pair of hinged shells around them.

For more than 300 million years, insect-like *trilobites* were very common. They scurried along the sea floor in search of food.

could protect themselves by rolling into a ball.

Other animals, called *crinoids*, were rooted to the sea floor by long stems. A crinoid's mouth sat within a cup at the stem's top. It was surrounded by five or more arms. Hairs in the arms and cup moved the nearby water to bring food into its mouth. *Brachiopods* also fed with the help of the fine tentacles inside their clam-like shells. Living crinoids and brachiopods can still be found today.

The Ordovician Period began about 500 million years ago and lasted about 70 million years. During this period, marine, or sea, animals lived in many new water environments. Life thrived in the warm tropical seas that covered northern Europe and the eastern United States.

Flower-like crinoids wiggled on their stalks, which were attached firmly to rocks on the sea bottom. Trilobites of all sizes appeared in most marine environments. A few corals also appeared. *Cephalopods*, the ancestors of the modern squid and octopus, were represented. Some cephalopods had cone-shaped shells from which their eyes and arms extended. Other types had curved shells, similar to the *chambered nautilus* that lives today.

An entirely new type of animal appeared early in the Ordovician Period: a primitive fish. It was the first true *vertebrate*, or animal with a backbone. The

Sponges lived in the last part of the Precambrian Era, some 700 million years ago. They represent one of the oldest and simplest forms of animal life.

Cephalopods introduced a new life-style in the Ordovician seas. They were active hunters, able to speed through the seas with special water jets. One straight-shelled cephalopod could grow twelve feet (3.6 meters) in length.

Life in the Ordovician seas included some forms still found in today's oceans, such as snails and corals. Trilobites (upper left), the spindly sea scorpion (middle left), and the multi-armed cephalopods (right and bottom left) ruled the sea floor.

bony plates that covered its body earned it the name *ostracoderm*, which means "shell-skinned." This early fish must have fed by plowing along the sea bottom, sifting through the mud with its round, jawless mouth. The stage was set for the Age of Fishes.

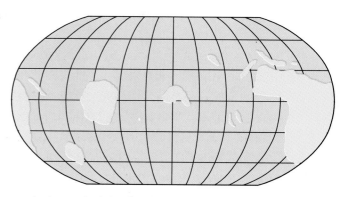

At the end of the Cambrian Period about 500 million years ago, landmasses straddled the equator.

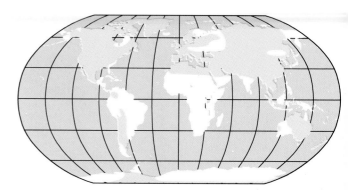

Today, deposits from the Cambrian and Ordovician Periods can be found in the tinted areas.

Fossils of this jawless fish are some 450 million years old. It had none of the control fins of modern fish and must have wriggled through the seas like a tadpole.

In the warm, shallow seas of the Silurian Period, coral reefs attracted all kinds of animals. A hungry cephalopod searches for a meal in this diorama.

The Age of Fishes

During the Silurian Period, between 430 and 395 million years ago, the lands that are now Africa and South America sat at Earth's South Pole. North America and parts of Europe were at the equator. Life thrived in the warm, shallow seas. Large coral reefs appeared and supported communities of marine plants and animals. Throughout the Silurian Period, primitive fish lived very successfully. Many different forms are known.

Placoderms ("plate-skinned" fish) appeared late in the Silurian Period. Bony plates around their bodies protected them. But like earlier fish, the skeletons inside their bodies were made of a soft material called *cartilage*. These fish carried a weapon no ostracoderm could match: the jaw. With improved swimming from pairs of fins, placoderms became very successful hunters.

For the more than three billion years in which life had been on Earth, it had remained locked in the oceans. In the warm, moist climate of the Silurian Period, life finally took to the land. Plants led the way.

When plants make their food by photosynthesis, they release oxygen gas. The plants during this time released oxygen into the oceans which rose into the atmosphere. High in the skies, some of the oxygen formed a layer of *ozone* gas. Ozone screens out the Sun's harmful rays. The creation of an ozone layer meant that life could now live on land.

Perhaps it began with small patches of algae on shoreline rocks, exposed to the air as tides rose and fell. Regardless of how it happened, the earliest known land plants appeared 410 million years ago. At first they clustered around the water's edge, but gradually they spread.

During the Devonian Period, between 395 and 345 million years ago, plants grew across the landscape. Toward the end of the Devonian Period, insects and arachnids first appeared. Living along the shoreline, primitive spiders, mites, and silverfish claimed the land for animals.

Near the end of the Devonian Period, two fish families replaced the placoderms. One, the bony fishes, developed internal skeletons of bone. The other, sharks and their relatives, had cartilage for their skeletons. These groups of fish still dominate the world's oceans.

Many volcanoes erupted in what is now England, Greenland, western Canada, and the Soviet Union. The world cli-

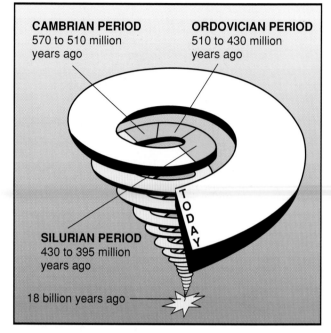

CAMBRIAN PERIOD
570 to 510 million years ago

ORDOVICIAN PERIOD
510 to 430 million years ago

SILURIAN PERIOD
430 to 395 million years ago

18 billion years ago

Over the millions of years of the Cambrian, Ordovician, and Silurian Periods, nature produced the backbone and jaw. The next step: the move onto land.

mate was generally drier than during the Silurian Period. But periods with little rain, or droughts, were often followed by very rainy periods.

The waters warmed. These warmer waters contained less oxygen, which fish needed to live. The fish in this period, like most fish today, breathed by taking oxygen from the water through their gills. With less oxygen in the water, many fish died.

Some fish, however, could gulp air from the surface. Their tiny blood vessels absorbed the oxygen. These fish were called *lungfish*. Lungfish can still be found living in Africa, South America, and Australia.

Relatives of this lobe-finned fish, a *coelacanth*, were the first vertebrates to tackle land. They were thought to be extinct until 1938, when one was caught off the coast of South Africa. This is one of the first photographs showing a coelacanth in its natural habitat.

One group of fish, the *lobe-fins*, could not only breath with lungs, but could stand on pairs of large fins. Using powerful muscles, they waddled from one pond to another. Lobe-fins were thought to be extinct. But in 1938, one member of the group, a *coelacanth*, was caught off the coast of South Africa.

One of the air-breathing lobe-finned fish, *Eusthenopteron*, could probably hold itself up on its fins. It would half-drag, half-waddle across the late Devonian landscape.

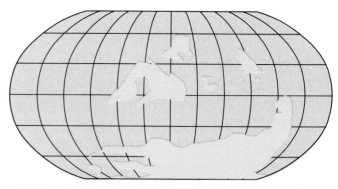

During the Devonian Period 390 million years ago, land that is now central Africa was at the South Pole. The equator cut through the single landmass that included North America and Europe.

Modern lungfish can be found in Australian, African, and South American rivers. Some have both lungs and gills, allowing them to breathe in or out of water. Others will drown if they can't reach the surface.

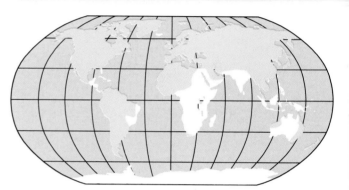

Today, fossils from the Silurian and Devonian Periods can be found in the tinted areas of the map.

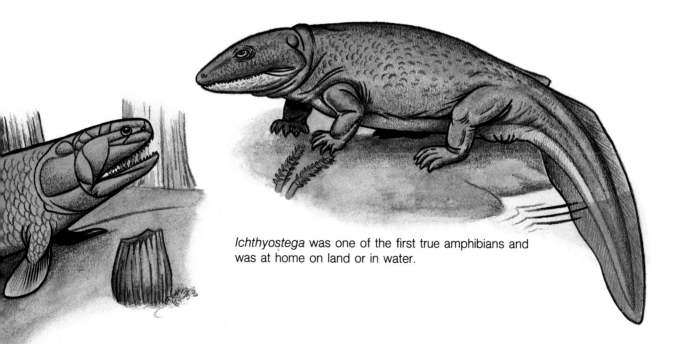

Ichthyostega was one of the first true amphibians and was at home on land or in water.

Early Life on Land

The climate turned warm and moist during the Carboniferous Period, 345 to 270 million years ago. This weather helped plants take over the land. Steamy lagoons supported giant club mosses, tree ferns, and relatives of today's horsetails. Farther inland, trees grew in thick forests that covered the lands that are now eastern North America and Europe.

These forests are what give the Carboniferous Period its name. Thick layers of dead plant matter, or vegetation, were buried in sediments. Over millions of years, pressure and heat turned the remains of the ancient forests into huge deposits of coal. Coal is called a fossil fuel because of this history.

Insects also thrived during the Carboniferous Period. The cockroach appeared

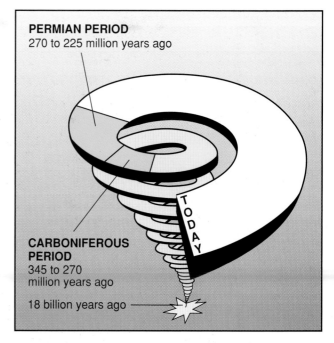

PERMIAN PERIOD
270 to 225 million years ago

CARBONIFEROUS
PERIOD
345 to 270
million years ago

18 billion years ago

TODAY

Amphibians and reptiles developed in the Carboniferous and Permian Periods, between 345 and 225 million years ago. They crawled the swamplands and forests that covered much of North America and Europe.

Insects thrive among the enormous tree ferns of a Carboniferous swamp. A giant dragonfly with a wingspan of nearly twenty inches (fifty centimeters) buzzes past a basking amphibian. At right, a human-sized millipede creeps toward a cockroach.

Giant ferns and club mosses were only some of the plant life of the Carboniferous Period. Shown here is a fossilized fern.

early on, scurrying along the rotted vegetation it used as food. Life took to the air as giant dragonflies—often with wingspans greater than one foot (thirty centimeters)—buzzed through the swamps. One of the strangest creatures was the giant *Artropleura*, a millipede-like animal up to five feet (1.5 meters) long.

Amphibians, the first four-legged animals, made their first appearance near

A trio of meat-eating *Cynognathus*, each about five-feet (1.5 meters) long, hunts down a *Kannemeyeria*. These mammal-like reptiles have been found in rocks from South Africa. Animals such as these are the ancestors of the first true mammals.

the end of the Devonian Period. But the group grew greatly in the warm and swampy Carboniferous Period. They arose from the air-breathing, lobe-finned fishes that briefly waddled across the Devonian shores. Like modern amphibians such as frogs and salamanders, they lived part of their lives on land and part in water. The early amphibians probably ate mostly fish and other aquatic animals. Even though they lived successful-ly, they were forced to live near the water's edge.

As the Carboniferous Period ended and the Permian Period began, the climate turned drier. Many landmasses were rising, draining the lagoons and swamps. As lakes and forests turned to deserts, many amphibian forms disappeared. To expand into the dry inland world, another type of animal appeared: the reptile.

Reptiles were the first creatures to live entirely on land. Amphibian eggs are held together by moist jelly and must be kept wet. Early reptiles were the first animals to lay eggs with shells. The shells kept the eggs from drying out and allowed reptiles to lay eggs away from water. Reptile life-forms exploded onto the scene. Whole new families of animals appeared to take advantage of the opportunities on land. One group became the ancestors of modern turtles and tortoises. Another group gave rise to both the "scaly reptiles," such as lizards and snakes, and the "ruling reptiles" including dinosaurs, flying reptiles, and their kin.

Yet another reptile group became the distant ancestor of mammals. One member of this group was *Dimetrodon*.

Thanks in part to the tough shells of their eggs, reptiles dominated the lands where amphibians could not survive. Dinosaurs, the best known reptiles, first appeared in the Mesozoic Era. The dinosaur hatchling pictured here lived in Australia about one hundred million years ago. When fully grown, this *Leaellynasaura* would be no larger than a chicken.

The folds of the Appalachian Mountains were thrust upward when the land that is now Africa rammed into North America some 250 million years ago.

A fierce meat-eater, Dimetrodon prowled the riverbanks of the southwestern U.S. some 250 million years ago. Like modern reptiles, Dimetrodon was ''cold-blooded''—it could not keep a constant body temperature. Dimetrodon may have used the skin ''sail'' on its back to help it warm up or cool down. Angling its sail to face the Sun would heat Dimetrodon up. Adjusting the sail away from the Sun would help it cool off.

Although Dimetrodon was not itself part of the line from which mammals developed, its group gave rise to ''mammal-like'' reptiles. These animals probably had fur and could control their body

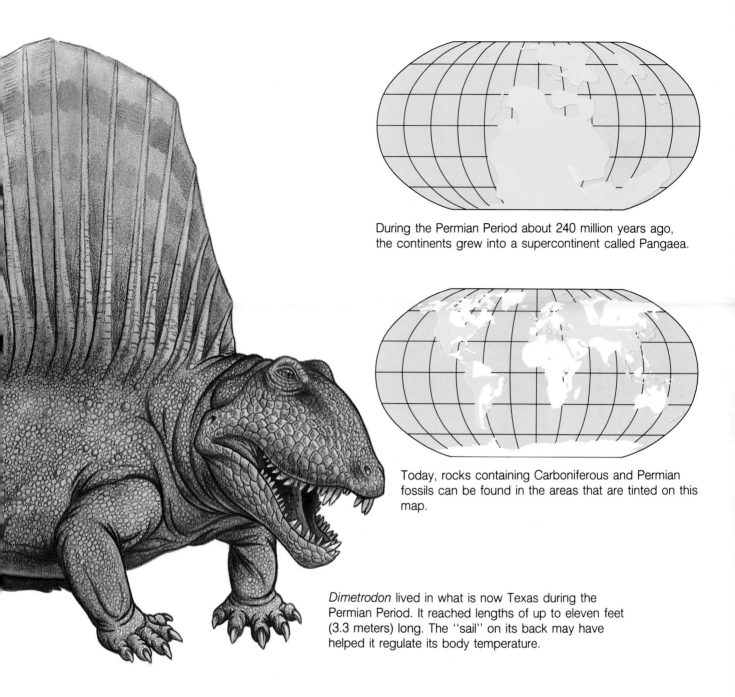

During the Permian Period about 240 million years ago, the continents grew into a supercontinent called Pangaea.

Today, rocks containing Carboniferous and Permian fossils can be found in the areas that are tinted on this map.

Dimetrodon lived in what is now Texas during the Permian Period. It reached lengths of up to eleven feet (3.3 meters) long. The "sail" on its back may have helped it regulate its body temperature.

temperatures as mammals do. They were the ancestors of the animals that, millions of years later, would be the first true mammals.

The continents, endlessly sliding over Earth's surface, continued a period of mountain-building that began during the Carboniferous Period. On the land that is now Asia, such grinding collisions created the Ural Mountains. At the close of the Permian Period, the land that is the eastern United States buckled to make the Appalachian Mountains. This was the result of a collision with Africa.

A beaked, pig-like *rhynchosaur* looks on as a *nothosaur* (bottom right) chases down a meal in a Triassic lagoon. Four-legged nothosaurs later gave rise to flippered *plesiosaurs* (middle).

The Mesozoic Era

The Rise of Reptiles

As the Paleozoic Era closed, the world's masses of land drew closer together. Around 240 million years ago the largest plates pressed together. They formed a single huge landmass which scientists call *Pangaea*. It was now possible for land animals and plants to move across large areas of land. Their move-

ment was limited only by the local climate. Not long after the start of the Mesozoic Era, Pangaea began splitting apart again to form the continents we know today.

Throughout the Mesozoic Era, the climate remained much warmer and drier than it is today. In fact, most of the era

Plateosaurus ("flat reptile") was the most common
early dinosaur scientists know of. Appearing late in the Triassic
Period, it was about twenty-six feet (eight meters) long. It walked
on four legs but may have stood on its hind legs to feed on treetops.

Protosuchus was a relative of modern crocodiles and an ancestor of
the dinosaurs. It was about thirty inches (76 centimeters) long.

had the warmest climates in the history
of life on Earth.

The mammal-like reptiles ruled the
world at the end of the Permian Period.
But another group was ready to take
over in the Triassic Period of the Mesozo
ic Era. From one line of small, lizard-like
animals, the *archosaurs* ("ruling reptiles") arose. All crocodiles, dinosaurs,
and flying reptiles developed from these
reptiles. Many early archosaurs looked
and acted much like modern crocodiles.
In fact, members of today's crocodile
family are the only surviving archosaurs.

The skull of *Camarasaurus* reveals its small head and long teeth. This sauropod roamed the western United States in Late Jurassic times.

It takes time and care to separate fossil dinosaur bones from the rock that protected them for millions of years.

By the end of the Triassic Period, all kinds of insect-eating, meat-eating, and plant-eating dinosaurs had arrived. Fossils of one early meat-eating dinosaur, *Coelophysis*, were found in New Mexico and Massachusetts. Coelophysis walked on either two or four legs. With a long neck and tail, it grew to about ten feet long (three meters) and probably ate small lizards. One of the most common plant-eaters was *Plateosaurus*. It roamed Triassic lagoons in what is now northern Europe.

By the opening of the Jurassic Period 190 million years ago, reptiles thrived on the land, in the sea, and in the air. Both the largest and the smallest of all dinosaurs lived during this time.

A *Brachiosaurus* skeleton at Chicago's Field Museum towers over its visitors. Brachiosaurus was one of the largest *sauropods*. Sauropods first appeared in the Jurassic Period and survived until the end of the reign of dinosaurs.

The largest and heaviest animals that ever lived were the *sauropods*. Gentle plant-eaters, they walked on four legs. Their huge, wide bodies had long, thin necks and tails. *Diplodocus*, the heavier *Apatosaurus* (incorrectly known as *Brontosaurus*), and the taller *Brachiosaurus* all stretched more than seventy feet (twenty-one meters) from head to tail. Full-grown brachiosaurs stood forty-five feet (13.7 meters) tall and weighed up to fifty tons (45.4 metric tons)!

Scientists found evidence of two even larger sauropods in the 1970s. These sauropods don't have official names, but from their sizes, the nicknames *Supersaurus* and *Ultrasaurus* seem to fit. If they were alive today, both could peer over the roof of a five-story building.

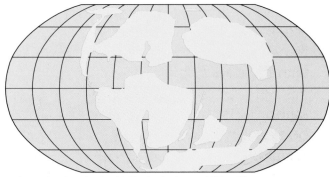

Late in the Jurassic Period about 135 million years ago, landmasses began to take on the shapes of the continents we know of today.

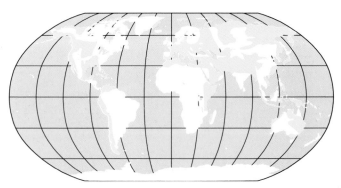

Today, fossils from the Triassic and Jurassic Periods are common in Africa, Asia, Australia, Europe, and the Americas.

The sauropods were the largest and heaviest reptiles that ever lived. Two recent discoveries, nicknamed *Supersaurus* and *Ultrasaurus*, grazed in what is now Colorado in Late Jurassic times. Ultrasaurus's front legs alone would be as tall as a modern giraffe.

Supersaurus

Ultrasaurus

Brachiosaurus

Human

Reptiles adapted to the seas as well. Sleek fish-like *ichthyosaurs* up to thirty-three feet (ten meters) long competed with the slower *plesiosaurs* for food. Fossils of ichthyosaurs show they had smooth, dark-colored skin on their upper bodies and light-colored skin on their lower bodies. Their large tails helped them become one of the swiftest hunters of the sea.

What plesiosaurs lacked in speed they made up for in length. Long-necked varieties reached forty feet (twelve meters). They probably spent most of their time near the surface, using their four flippers to glide through the water in search of fish.

Many dinosaurs developed protective armor. This plant-eating *Stegosaurus* roamed the western United States late in the Jurassic Period. Up to twenty-five feet (7.6 meters) long, the animal had a spiked tail and bony plates. The plates may have helped Stegosaurus maintain its body temperature.

Reptiles also took to the Jurassic skies. Late in the Triassic Period, some lizard-like reptiles developed a web of skin connecting their legs to their bodies. This skin allowed them to glide through the air between trees. From these gliding lizards came the Jurassic *pterosaurs* ("winged reptiles").

Pterosaurs first appeared about 200 million years ago. More than eighty species are known. Some were insect-eaters no larger than modern birds. Others were giant scavengers that were the largest animals ever to fly. Some of the pterosaurs had fur.

About 150 million years ago, a new group took flight. The crow-sized animal had a beak, sharp teeth, claws extending from its wings, and feathers. *Archaeopteryx* ("ancient wing") is the first recorded bird. Only six fossils of these birds have been found. All come from sediments in Germany in an area that was once a Jurassic lagoon.

The Jurassic seas of Europe were home to some strange creatures. The long-necked *Plesiosaurus* was about ten feet (three meters) long. It moved through the water with paddle-like legs and feet. The sleek, fish-like ichthyosaur called *Stenopterygius* was about five feet (1.5 meters) long.

Rhamphorhynchus (top) was a long-tailed flying reptile about twenty-four inches (61 centimeters) long. *Archaeopteryx* (center) was the first creature known to have feathers. Except for its feathers, Archaeopteryx fossils look much like those of the small meat-eating *Compsognathus* (bottom). Many scientists believe that birds developed from relatives of such small two-legged dinosaurs.

Twilight of the Dinosaurs

During the Cretaceous Period between 135 and 65 million years ago, South America began splitting from Africa. The Atlantic Ocean opened and widened and the climate cooled. The dinosaur population grew to its largest yet.

The cooler weather helped to spread an enormous amount of plant life throughout the world. Flowering plants first appeared in the Cretaceous Period.

These plants protected their seeds within a special casing—a *fruit*. Magnolias were one of the earliest flowering plants. Modern trees such as the oak, aspen, poplar, and sequoia all have ancestors that first appeared during the Cretaceous Period.

True birds, the descendants of Archaeopteryx, developed throughout the Cretaceous Period. Flying reptiles grew

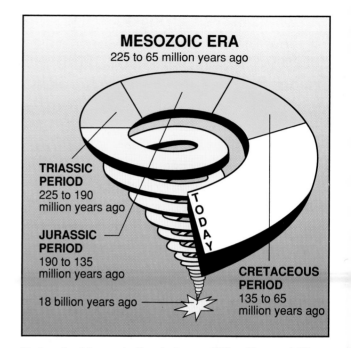

MESOZOIC ERA
225 to 65 million years ago

TRIASSIC PERIOD
225 to 190 million years ago

JURASSIC PERIOD
190 to 135 million years ago

18 billion years ago →

TODAY

CRETACEOUS PERIOD
135 to 65 million years ago

During the Mesozoic Era, between 225 million and 65 million years ago, reptiles ruled the world.

Several giant pterosaurs circle a dead *Alamosaurus*. The largest animal ever to fly, this pterosaur—*Quetzalcoatlus*—had wings that stretched nearly forty-three feet (twelve meters).

Flowering plants became dominant during the Cretaceous Period. Magnolias (left) were among the first. Relatives of modern trees, such as the oak (center) and the aspen (right), also appeared.

to their largest size. The *Pteranodon* sported wings over twenty-four feet (seven meters) across while its body was only about the size of a turkey. Pteranodon launched itself into the wind from cliff-side roosts and skimmed the sea in search of fish.

Until the 1970s, scientists believed that Pteranodons were the largest of the flying reptiles. Then scientists in Texas unearthed *Quetzalcoatlus*. A giant pterosaur, its wings stretched over forty-three feet (twelve meters) across. It is the largest creature ever to fly. Like modern vultures, it fed off the flesh of whatever dead animals it could find.

The *hadrosaurs* were among the gentlest dinosaurs. They appeared in the Late Cretaceous Period and ranged across what is now the Americas, Europe, and Asia. Also known as "duck-billed" dinosaurs for their flat, toothless snouts, hadrosaurs averaged about thirty feet (9.1 meters) in length. They walked about on two legs in a stooped position, frequently dropping to all four feet. Webs of skin between their toes suggest they were good swimmers. They probably nibbled on water plants growing at the edges of freshwater ponds.

Corythosaurus is one of the largest hadrosaurs, also called duck-billed dinosaurs because of their flat, toothless beaks. Over thirty-three feet (ten meters) long, Corythosaurus had a high, narrow crest atop its head.

The giant sea turtle *Archelon* takes some interest in a passing cephalopod. Some thirteen feet (four meters) long, Archelon was the largest turtle ever.

44

Tyrannosaurus (right) was the most fearsome killer of its time. Up to fifty feet (fifteen meters) long, it held its huge head twenty feet (six meters) above the ground. *Triceratops* (left) normally kept far from meat-eaters. If cornered, though, its head frill and horns gave Triceratops a fighting chance.

The hadrosaurs are very much alike from the neck down. But the bony crests atop their skulls vary quite a bit. The crests of some are solid bone. Others, such as *Corythosaurus*, contain winding nasal passages. These spaces probably served to make Corythosaurus's calls to one another louder.

Most of the stegosaurs became extinct in the Early Cretaceous Period. But

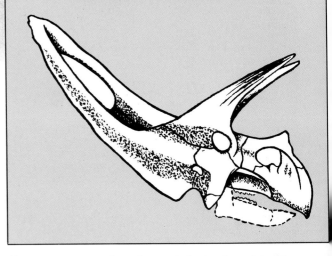

Torosaurus was a three-horned plant-eater related to *Triceratops*. Its huge frill gave Torosaurus the largest head of any known land animal—8.5 feet (2.4 meters) long.

another well-known group of armored plant-eaters thrived. These were the *ceratopsians* (''horned faces''). Animals such as *Torosaurus*, *Triceratops*, and *Styracosaurus* were protected by horny spikes on their faces and a bony frill around their heads. The frill of Torosaurus was the largest of all. Its skull with the frill measured up to 8.5 feet (2.6 meters) long.

Triceratops, the last and largest of the ceratopsians, was a brute in its own right. The animal grew up to thirty-six feet

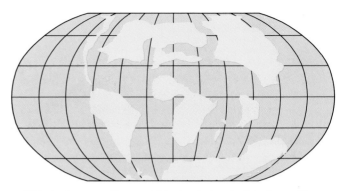

This is the way the world looked about sixty-five million years ago. South America separated from Africa during the Cretaceous Period, widening the Atlantic Ocean.

This scene was frozen into a fossil found in 1971. The beak of a *Protoceratops* had pierced the chest of an attacking *Velociraptor*. The Velociraptor's large toe claw had slashed the belly of its prey. They must have died at the same time.

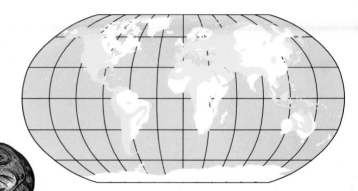

Fossils from the Cretaceous Period have been found in the tinted areas on this map.

Mosasaurs were true marine lizards that ranged around the world by the end of the Cretaceous Period. Up to thirty-feet (9.1 meters) long, *Tylosaurus* was a fearsome predator in the sea that once covered Kansas.

(eleven meters) long. The two long horns above its eyes were up to three feet (one meter) in length. Even a very hungry meat-eater would get out of the way of a charging Triceratops. Triceratops often fought with its own kind, perhaps to defend its home territory. Fossils show scars on their bony frills and horns where their wounds healed.

With the powerful meat-eaters that roamed the Cretaceous world, such defenses were necessary. A quick drink from a lake or river could turn deadly as *Phobosuchus*, the fifty-foot-long (fifteen meters) "horror crocodile," lashed out for a meal. It was the biggest crocodile that ever lived.

The most frightening and perhaps the best known meat-eater also appeared during this time: Tyrannosaurus. This monster's powerful jaws were lined with seven-inch-long (eighteen centimeters) teeth. It stood on two muscular legs with its head thrust forward. Its mouth was so large that, if one were alive today, it could probably swallow a human whole. Yet its tiny forelegs seem too small to have been of any help in hunting or grasping prey. Their real use is still unknown.

What food did this giant killer eat? It couldn't have eaten the great sauropods like Brachiosaurus. They had already been extinct for millions of years by the time Tyrannosaurus appeared. Instead, it preyed on the many small plant-eaters that lived alongside it in western North America.

The small meat-eaters of the Cretaceous could be just as deadly as tyrannosaurs. Six-foot-long (1.8 meters) *Velociraptor* ("swift robber"), for example, raced after its victims and raked them with a huge, curved toe claw. Velociraptors hunted in packs and worked together to bring down large animals. As the animals stalked their prey, they were able to hold their knife-like claws off the ground. During an attack, they flexed their toe claws downward and slashed at their prey. A fossil was discovered in 1971 of a Velociraptor as it attacked a plant-eating *Protoceratops*.

During the Cretaceous Period, dinosaurs in the area that is now Australia lived in a cool polar climate. This painting shows seven small dinosaurs found in Australia. All but Muttaburrasaurus lived in the polar region. Their small size may have been an adaptation to the cool, dark conditions. Leaellynasaura was a chicken-sized plant-eater, while the armored ankylosaur was about the size of a sheep. The meat-eating dwarf allosaur was no taller than a human.

Dinosaurs, pterosaurs, aquatic reptiles, and many plants died off at the end of the Cretaceous Period. This provided new opportunities for the small mammals that had been around since the Jurassic Period.

The Great Extinction

Dinosaurs ruled the Earth for 140 million years. Then, suddenly, they disappeared from the fossil record. No one is exactly certain what killed them off. Everything from exploding stars to digestive problems has been proposed to explain it.

Most of these ideas focus only on the dinosaurs. Many other groups also vanished as the Cretaceous Period came to a close. The group of flying reptiles, the pterosaurs, were wiped out completely. The sea-going reptiles—ichthyosaurs, plesiosaurs, and others—vanished from the oceans. *Ammonites* and *belemnites*, cephalopods that had been swimming in the ancient seas long before dinosaurs, also disappeared.

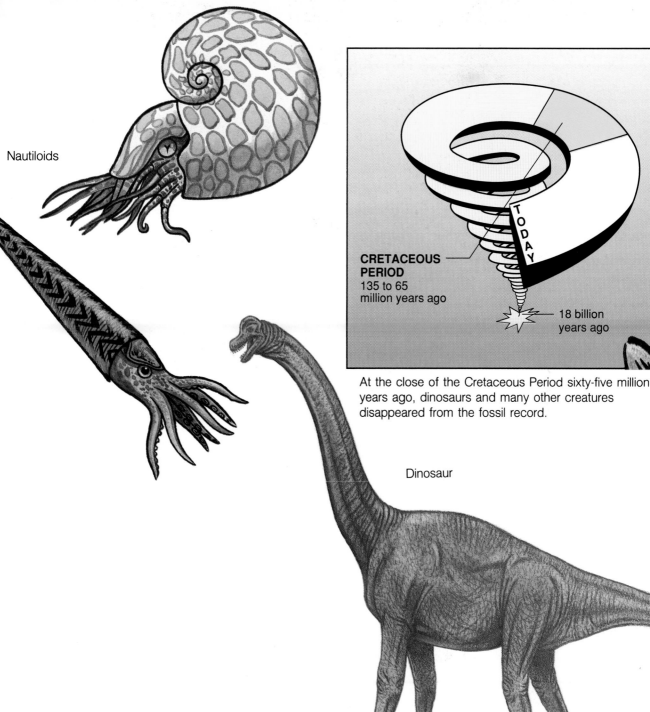

Nautiloids

CRETACEOUS
PERIOD
135 to 65
million years ago

TODAY

18 billion
years ago

At the close of the Cretaceous Period sixty-five million years ago, dinosaurs and many other creatures disappeared from the fossil record.

Dinosaur

In fact, about half of the plant and animal species on the Earth died off. Why?

In 1980, a group of scientists made an announcement about a layer of clay formed at the end of the Cretaceous Period. The clay contained the element *iridium* at levels 160 times higher than normal. The element is rare in Earth's crust but is common in meteorites. The scientists suggested that Earth was struck by a giant meteorite about six miles (ten kilometers) across. The effects of this huge impact, they argued, would have changed the Earth and its atmosphere so greatly that many living things would have died.

Evidence of past collisions with meteorites lies within more than 100 craters scientists have identified on Earth. Shown here is the peaceful Earth before an impact.

Streaking through the atmosphere at incredible speeds, an asteroid six miles (10 kilometers) across is surrounded by hot, glowing air.

Geologists at first resisted this idea. All the known craters were not big or old enough to be the site of such an impact. Geologists pointed to other changes that could have affected living things. Oceans were widening as the continents moved toward their present positions. Huge flows of lava erupted from volcanoes in India at the end of the Cretaceous Period. How might this have affected the environment?

Astronomers came up with more evidence to support their theory. On average, they said, Earth is struck by giant meteorites every ten million years. They knew that geologists had found deformed ("shocked") quartz crystals and tiny glass spheres in the clay. These would be produced if a giant meteorite had hit Earth. They wondered if perhaps the crater was buried by sediments on the ocean floor. Perhaps it was erased by the movement of continents.

Then, in the 1980s geologists confirmed what the astronomers had suspected. They discovered a huge crater buried along the coast of Mexico's Yucatan Peninsula. The crater is more than sixty-eight miles (110 kilometers) across. Today, most geologists accept this as proof that a huge meteorite slammed into Earth sixty-five million years ago.

How would this have killed off the dinosaurs? A meteorite of this size would

Slamming into the Earth with the force of a million tons of explosives, the meteorite splashes into the ocean floor. Tons of water, rock, and dust are blasted high into the atmosphere.

Meteor Crater in Arizona was created 50,000 years ago when a meteorite just 150 feet (46 meters) across crashed into the desert. The crater itself is 600 feet (183 meters) deep and 4,100 feet (1,250 meters) across.

have struck the Earth's crust with incredible force. Scientists think the blast carved out the crater and a brilliant fireball grew from the point of the impact. Its searing heat started great forest fires. An enormous cloud of gas and dust shot high into the atmosphere. Spreading around the world, the dust blocked the Sun's light. The earth was plunged into months of darkness and near-freezing temperatures. Plants died off, which killed the plant-eating animals. Then the meat-eating animals died too. Acid rains caused by gases in the cloud may have polluted the seas, weakening the shells of many marine animals and causing their deaths.

It is possible that some dinosaurs might have survived these effects. During the Cretaceous Period, there were some dinosaurs that were already used to cold and dark conditions. Australia was near the South Pole during the Cretaceous Period. Scientists there have found many small dinosaurs with large eyes. Large eyes may have helped these dinosaurs see during the winter months when the Sun did not rise at all. Some scientists find it hard to believe that a few months of darkness from the cloud of a meteorite impact could have killed these dinosaurs. Information like this creates many questions. To this day, no one is certain what caused the mass extinction of life in the Cretaceous Period.

During the Cenozoic Era, the modern horse arose from a fox-sized ancestor (left). Saber-toothed cats (right bottom) appeared later on. *Megatherium*, the largest ground sloth (center), *Glyptodon*, the giant armadillo (rear left), and the wooly rhinoceros (right top) came on the scene more recently.

The Cenozoic Era
The Age of Mammals

Throughout the 140-million-year rule of the giant reptiles, mammals were no larger than mice. Reptiles may have kept the tiny mammals scurrying. They simply may have had no chance to develop into larger creatures.

When opportunity came, however, the mammals were ready. Within ten million years after the extinction of the dinosaurs, mammals of every size appeared. Rodents, whales, early horses, camels, pigs, bats, and rhinos were all present.

One key to the success of the mammals was a change in the way they bore their young. Instead of laying eggs like most of the reptiles, the ancient mammals began bearing their young live. In the southern areas, animals were born at a very early stage of development. The newborns moved to a pouch on their

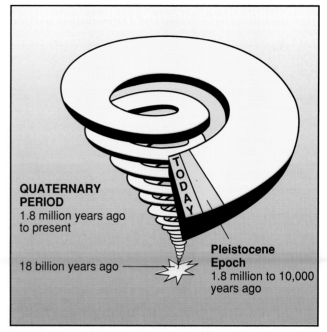

Between 1.8 million and 10,000 years ago, glaciers made several advances across the Pleistocene landscape.

About fifty million years ago, this *Mioplosus* choked on its meal as it tried to swallow another fish. The scene was captured in a fossil found by scientists.

mother's belly where they fed on her milk. They stayed in the pouch until they were large enough to fend for themselves. These were the first *marsupials*. Modern marsupials include the kangaroo and opossum.

Marsupials thrived on the landmass that was South America and Australia. The two continents split apart during the Cretaceous Period, and the marsupials were separated. They developed differently on the two continents, taking advantage of all the environments the dinosaurs had left behind. This was especially true in Australia, where marsupials lived in every available area.

Northern mammals did things a little differently. They held their young within their bodies in an internal "pouch." Nutrients and oxygen—things the baby

Standing eighteen feet (5.5 meters) tall, *Baluchitherium* was the world's biggest rhinoceros and the largest land mammal known to have ever lived.

needed to grow—were passed from the mother's blood to the unborn young. Most modern mammals including humans develop in this way.

Some animals we don't usually think of as North American had relatives there. For example, the camel family developed in North America. Forty million years ago, the oldest-known member of the camel family appeared. It was a beast not much larger than a jackrabbit. About three million years ago, many members of this group moved to what is now South America and Asia. Most American camels died out a few thousand years ago. Today their only living relatives are the llama and alpaca of South America.

Members of the rhinoceros family roamed North America until about three million years ago. The earliest rhinos were small, quick, and hornless. One species was about the size of a pig. It traveled the western United States in herds of thousands. At the other extreme was the giant rhinoceros, *Baluchitherium*. Able to nibble branches twenty-feet off the ground, it was the world's largest known land mammal. It traveled Asia in small herds some thirty million years ago.

The ancestors of modern horses can be traced back some fifty million years to a fox-sized animal living in North America and Europe. About five million years ago the modern horse arose in North America. It quickly moved into Asia and spread further to Africa and Europe. The horses in the Americas died out about ten thousand years ago. Those in

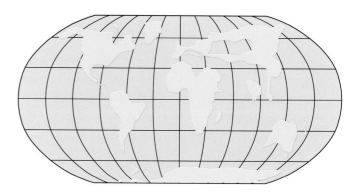

During the Tertiary Period, between sixty-five million and 1.8 million years ago, the continents approached their present positions. Shown here is the world about thirty-five million years ago.

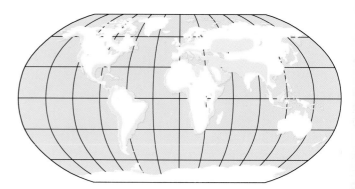

Early Cenozoic deposits have been found in the tinted areas of this map.

Birds and mammals were rivals in the Tertiary Period. In South America and Antarctica, the largest meat-eaters were a group of flightless birds called *phororhacids*. The six-foot-tall birds disappeared about three million years ago. Their North American relative *Diatryma*—pictured here—was not as successful.

the Americas today were brought over by European explorers in the 1500s.

Birds had also survived the Cretaceous extinction. About forty million years ago a new type of meat-eating bird appeared in Antarctica and South America: the *phororhacids*. Over six feet (two meters) tall, these large-beaked, flightless birds ruled their lands. They were swift runners. Chasing down a marsupial meal, these birds probably held their prey with one foot and tore it apart with their beaks.

Similar predatory birds developed in Europe and North America. One, called *Diatryma*, lived in Wyoming about thirty million years ago. These birds were not as successful as their relatives in South America. They competed with the mammals of the day for rule of their lands. Eventually, the mammals won.

About five million years ago, when North and South America were separate landmasses, volcanos began building up the Isthmus of Panama. A land bridge formed, and the meat-eating mammals of the north invaded the south. They wiped out all but a few of the South American marsupials. Today only the opossum survives. As Antarctica slid toward its present position and began icing over, the climate turned cooler and drier. The phororhacids and their relatives slowly died off.

A pair of harmless *Uintatheriums* startles a group of early horses. These horses were about the size of a modern fox. They lived in North America and Europe about fifty million years ago.

Ten million years ago, the Great Plains
of the United States was a vast
savanna teeming with grazing animals.
''Shovel-tusked'' *mastodons* (right rear)
fed on water plants. They shared the
wetlands with aquatic rhinos and pig-like
oreodonts (right). *Synthetoceras*, sport-
ing a Y-shaped horn on its snout (left
front), and the clawed sloth-like *Moropus*
(left) join horses and other animals.

Advance of the Glaciers

The cooling climate of the Tertiary Period turned into the great Ice Ages. Between about 1.8 million and ten thousand years ago, a period called the Pleistocene Epoch, glaciers and ice sheets advanced over the continents four or five times.

No one knows exactly what caused the great Ice Ages. But it is certain that slight changes in the Earth's yearly orbit around the Sun had some effect. The glaciers surged forward in the cold weather, and moved back as the climate warmed. They advanced again when the cold returned. The last Ice Age was twenty thousand years ago. Vast ice sheets more than two miles (3.2 kilometers) thick stretched as far south as the midwestern United States and central Europe. So much water was locked up in the ice that world sea levels dropped by more than 350 feet (106 meters).

During the cool periods, heavy snows fell in Earth's polar areas. Over time, the snow deepened to about one hundred feet (thirty meters). Its sheer weight turned the bottom layers to ice.

The ice sheet that covers Greenland is a reminder of Earth's great Ice Ages. Even today, the ice at the center of Greenland is ten thousand feet (2.9 kilometers) thick. Great rivers of ice flow toward the sea, where they melt and break off as icebergs.

Slowly, the ice sheet, or *glacier*, began moving downhill. Boulders frozen into its bottom layer raked across the landscape. They polished, scratched, and ground the rock over which they moved.

The last ice sheet melted away some ten thousand years ago. In places where the ice was thickest, Earth's crust is still reacting today. Near the shores of Lake Superior in North America, the land is

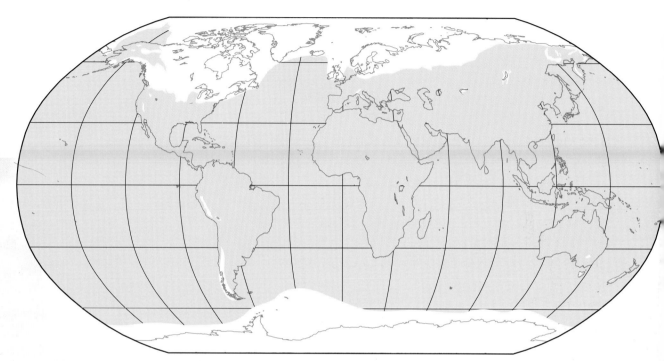

Some twenty thousand years ago, at the height of the last Ice Age, vast Arctic ice sheets stretched as far south as central Europe and the midwestern United States.

Fragments of a retreating ice sheet splash into a deep glacial lake. The great ice sheets grew more than a mile (1.6 kilometers) thick. As they moved, they slowly scoured and scarred landscape.

Saber-toothed cats first appeared
thirty million years ago. *Smilodon*,
the last and largest of them,
was built more powerfully than a
modern lion.

rising by about fifteen inches (thirty-eight centimeters) per century. It is slowly bouncing back from the ice sheet's crushing weight.

Many scientists believe that we are now enjoying the warm period between two ice ages. Thousands of years from now, the ice may return.

Fossils of most of the mammal species now living in Europe have been found within Pleistocene sediments. A rich source of fossils are the solid asphalt pools known as *tar pits*. Animals that stumbled into the thick, black tar sank and were trapped. Once the tar turned solid, it protected the bones of its victims.

The mammals that lived during the Tertiary Period developed into some strange forms during the Pleistocene Ep-

Protected from the cold by a thick coat of wool and hair, herds of mammoths roamed Europe, Asia, and North America. Up to thirteen feet (four meters) high at the shoulders, they were slightly larger than modern elephants.

och. Saber-toothed cats first appeared early in the Tertiary Period and they survived into the Pleistocene. The group's largest member, *Smilodon*, was the last of its group. Larger and more powerful

Stumbling into a thick pool of asphalt, a mammoth desperately struggles to free itself. Predators looking for an easy meal become trapped. Tar pits are a rich source of Ice Age fossils.

than a modern lion, Smilodon's most unusual features were two enormous teeth. With these teeth, Smilodon could rip through the thickest hides of the time. Living in North America and Europe, it probably fed on large plant-eaters. As the animals it fed upon died off, so did the last of the saber-toothed cats.

With the onset of colder weather, many animals developed thick, hairy hides. The *woolly rhinoceros*, for example, roamed North America, Europe, and northern Asia. The *woolly mammoth* is probably the best known Ice Age mammal. Tracking through the snow-covered lands in large herds, the mammoth weighed nearly twice as much as modern elephants. Shaggy, black hair covered its body. Great upward-curling tusks grew from its face. It stood some thirteen feet tall (four meters) and measured nearly twenty-four feet (over seven meters) from tusk to tail.

The giant ground sloth *Megatherium* lived in South America. Up to eighteen feet (5.5 meters) long, this ancestor of today's sloths walked on four legs. It reared up to full height to reach the leaves it fed upon. Another South American mammal was an ancestor of the modern armadillo. Living in roughly the same area as Megatherium, the giant *Glyptodon* was up to nine feet (2.7 meters) long.

Like the great reptiles before them, some mammals adapted to life in the water. The largest of the ancient whales was *Basilosaurus*. It grew to up to seventy feet (21.3 meters) long. A powerful tail made up much of this length. Like all of

Basilosaurus, the largest of an early family of whales (left), lived forty million years ago. Modern whales and dolphins developed from its relatives.

the ancient whales, Basilosaurus had a pair of hind legs. Its legs were just two feet (0.6 meter) long and remained hidden under its thick flesh. All modern whales descended from these relatives. Today the blue whale is the largest of all living animals, reaching lengths of ninety-eight feet (30 meters). This may be larger than any dinosaur ever was.

Early *primates* had arrived in the early Tertiary Period. This is the family in which scientists place apes, chimpanzees, and human beings. As the Tertiary forests gave way to Pleistocene grasslands, some of these primates were ready for the climb toward humanity. Early humans would soon appear.

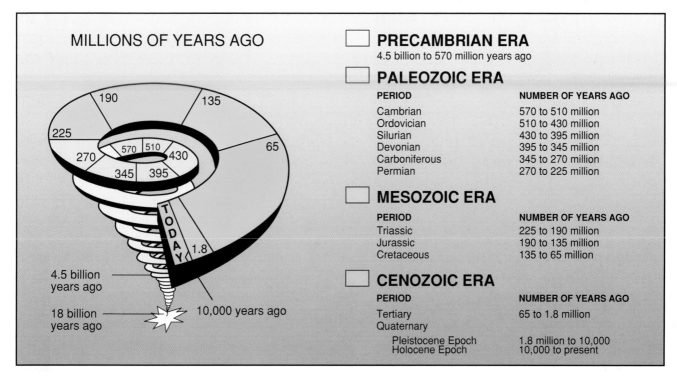

This time spiral shows the span of Earth's history. The entire fossil record so far represents a mere 13 percent of Earth's whole story.

Megaloceros, a giant deer, lived in Ireland during the Ice Age. Its antlers spanned more than ten feet (three meters).

Index